MASTERING BALANCE

A Modern Guide to Harmonizing Work and Life

Nicole Varela Rodriguez

To my family, whose unwavering belief in me has given me the courage to believe in myself.

To my parents, who have supported me through every wild idea without hesitation.

To my life coach, for gifting me the journal that illuminated my path.

And to all who have touched my life in countless ways...it is because of you that this book exists.

CONTENTS

INTRODUCTION

In today's fast-paced world, the quest for work-life balance has become more critical than ever. With the increasing demands of careers, family, and personal growth, finding harmony between professional and personal lives can feel like an elusive goal. Yet, mastering this balance is essential for achieving both long-term success and personal fulfillment.

Work-life balance isn't just about splitting time evenly between work and home. It's about creating a rhythm that allows you to thrive in all areas of life, without sacrificing health, happiness, or productivity. This guide is designed to help you redefine your approach to balance, break down misconceptions, and provide you with practical strategies to take control of your time and energy.

Let's embark on this journey together, exploring ways to reclaim your time, nurture your well-being, and ultimately, master the art of balance.

The Importance of Work-Life Balance

Work-life balance is more than just a buzzword; it is a crucial component of overall well-being and productivity. Striking the right balance between professional obligations and personal fulfillment can lead to numerous benefits, including improved mental and physical health, increased job satisfaction, and stronger relationships with family and friends.

A balanced life directly impacts not only your physical and mental health but also your productivity and satisfaction at work and home. Burnout, stress, and fatigue can hinder success and make it challenging to stay connected with loved ones and personal passions. This guide explores why work-life balance is vital for well-being and how embracing it can lead to a more meaningful and enjoyable life.

How This Guide Can Help

"Mastering Balance: A Modern Guide to Harmonizing Work and Life" is designed to be your comprehensive companion in navigating the complexities of balancing career demands with personal aspirations. Whether you're an overworked professional, a busy parent, or someone simply looking to enhance your quality of life, this guide offers practical strategies and actionable insights to help you achieve equilibrium.

In the following chapters, you'll find a wealth of information on:

- Understanding Work-Life Balance: Defining what balance means and addressing common myths and misconceptions.
- Time Management Techniques: Effective methods to help you organize your schedule and boost productivity.
- Setting Boundaries: Strategies to delineate work and personal time effectively.
- Managing Stress: Techniques for reducing stress and preventing burnout.
- Building Support Systems: The importance of having a

network of support from family, friends, and colleagues.

Through a combination of expert advice, practical tips, and self-assessment tools, this guide is crafted to help you identify areas of imbalance and make meaningful adjustments. By applying the principles outlined in this book, you will be better equipped to create a balanced life where work and personal happiness can thrive together.

Embark on this journey towards a more balanced life with us and discover how mastering this equilibrium can lead to greater fulfillment and success both at work and beyond.

CHAPTER 1: UNDERSTANDING WORK-LIFE BALANCE

In this chapter, we dive into what work-life balance truly means. Many of us struggle with balancing our careers, personal lives, and health, often feeling overwhelmed by the demands on our time and energy. Here, we'll explore the real definition of work-life balance and clear up common myths and misconceptions that might be holding you back. We'll also examine how an imbalance can impact your health and productivity, laying the foundation for the practical strategies that follow in later chapters. By understanding the core principles of balance, you'll be better prepared to start making meaningful changes in your life.

Defining Work-Life Balance

At its core, work-life balance refers to the equilibrium between professional responsibilities and personal life. For some, it might mean working fewer hours; for others, it could be about integrating personal passions into a demanding career. It's about finding a harmony that allows you to meet your professional responsibilities while still prioritizing your health, relationships, and personal growth.

Work-life balance is a dynamic and individualized state. It is less about achieving a perfect, static equilibrium and more about continuously adjusting and finding harmony based on current life circumstances and priorities. It involves recognizing that some days, work may take precedence, while other days, personal time and self-care are the priority. The key is not perfection, but the pursuit of a balance that feels right for you.

By understanding what balance truly means, you'll be equipped to start creating a lifestyle that supports both your career ambitions and personal well-being.

Common Myths and Misconceptions

Despite its importance, work-life balance is often surrounded by misconceptions that can hinder our pursuit of it. Let's debunk some of the most common myths:

1. Myth: Work-Life Balance Means Equal Time for Work and Personal Life Many believe that work-life balance requires a 50/50 split between professional and personal activities. In reality, balance is not about dividing time equally but about managing priorities and making conscious choices. For example, during a busy period at work, you might invest more time professionally, while during personal events or crises, you might shift focus to your personal life.

2. Myth: Achieving Work-Life Balance Means Never Working Overtime. While balance aims to prevent burnout, it doesn't necessarily mean you'll never work late or take on extra tasks. The key is to ensure that such periods are manageable and temporary and that they

don't consistently infringe on your time or well-being.

3. Myth: Only People with Flexible Jobs Can Achieve Work-Life Balance Although flexible work arrangements can facilitate balance, it's not the only path. People with rigid schedules or traditional job roles can also achieve balance through effective time management, setting boundaries, and prioritizing self-care.

4. Myth: Work-Life Balance Is a One-Time Achievement Work-life balance is not a destination but an ongoing process. Life circumstances, work demands, and personal priorities evolve, requiring continuous adjustments. Regular reflection and recalibration are essential to maintaining balance over time.

Practical Tip: Focus on Quality, Not Quantity. Instead of stressing over the exact number of hours spent on work versus personal activities, aim to be fully present in whatever you're doing. Quality time - whether it's a focused work session or a moment of relaxation with loved ones - is more valuable than attempting to split your day evenly. Small but mindful actions, like taking a real lunch break or turning off work notifications during family time, can significantly improve your sense of balance.

The Impact on Health and Productivity

Understanding the significance of work-life balance extends beyond personal fulfillment; it has profound implications for both health and productivity:

Health Benefits:

- Reduced Stress: Achieving balance helps mitigate chronic stress, which is linked to numerous health issues such as cardiovascular diseases, anxiety, and depression.

- Improved Mental Health: Engaging in personal activities and leisure can enhance mood, reduce feelings of burnout, and promote a sense of well-being.
- Better Physical Health: A balanced lifestyle often includes time for exercise and healthy eating, which are critical for maintaining overall physical health.

Productivity Gains:

- Enhanced Focus: When you manage your time well and avoid overworking, you can improve your concentration and efficiency during work hours.
- Increased Creativity: Regular breaks and time for personal interests can foster creativity and problem-solving skills, contributing to better work performance.
- Greater Job Satisfaction: A balanced approach often leads to higher job satisfaction and lower turnover rates, as employees feel valued and supported.

Achieving work-life balance is not about perfection but about finding a personalized equilibrium that works for you. By dispelling myths and understanding the profound impact balance has on your health and productivity, you can embark on a journey to integrate both professional and personal aspects of your life more harmoniously.

In the subsequent chapters, we will explore practical strategies and tools to help you assess your current balance, set achievable goals, and implement effective techniques to create a more fulfilling and balanced life.

CHAPTER 2: ASSESSING YOUR CURRENT BALANCE

Before you can make meaningful changes to your work-life balance, it's essential to understand where you currently stand. Many of us go through the motions without taking the time to reflect on how we spend our days, often feeling overwhelmed without knowing exactly why. Self-assessment is a crucial first step in identifying areas of imbalance and recognizing patterns that may be hindering your overall well-being.

This stage is about taking a closer look at your daily routines, habits, and priorities. By using simple self-assessment tools, you can uncover where your time and energy are going and where they might need to be redirected. Once you identify these imbalances, you can start setting realistic personal goals that align with your vision of a balanced life. This awareness lays the foundation for the strategies and adjustments that will help you create a more harmonious routine.

Self-Assessment Tools

◆ ◆ ◆

To evaluate your current work-life balance, start with a self-assessment. This involves reflecting on various aspects of your life to determine how well you are managing both professional and personal responsibilities.

Here are some effective self-assessment tools:

- Complete a detailed Work-Life Balance Questionnaire to evaluate different dimensions of your life. Questions might include:
    - How satisfied are you with your current work schedule?
    - Do you have enough time for family and personal activities?
    - Are you frequently stressed or overwhelmed by work demands?
- Time Tracking Keep a time log for a week, recording how much time you spend on work, family, personal activities, and rest. Analyze this log to see where your time is concentrated and whether you are allocating sufficient time to non-work activities.
- Stress and Satisfaction Surveys Use surveys to measure your stress levels and overall satisfaction with various aspects of your life. Tools like the Perceived Stress Scale (PSS) and Job Satisfaction Surveys can provide insights into how well you manage work-related stress and personal contentment.
- Energy Audit Assess your energy levels throughout the day. Identify periods when you feel most energetic and periods when you feel drained. This can help you understand how well your current balance supports your productivity and well-being.

Practical Tip: Begin your self-assessment journey with a simple, daily check-in. At the end of each day, take five minutes to jot down how you spent your time and how you felt during key activities. Note what energized you and what left you feeling drained. This quick habit can provide immediate insights and set the stage for deeper assessments, helping you identify patterns and areas for improvement without feeling overwhelmed.

Identifying Imbalances

❖ ❖ ❖

Once you have gathered information through self-assessment tools, the next step is to identify areas of imbalance.

Common indicators of imbalance include:

1. Work Overload If you find yourself consistently working late into the evening or bringing work home, this could signal an imbalance. Overworking can lead to stress and interfere with personal time.
2. Neglected Personal Time Assess whether you are missing out on important personal activities, such as spending time with family, engaging in hobbies, or practicing self-care. A lack of personal time often indicates that work demands overshadow personal needs.
3. Physical and Emotional Symptoms Pay attention to physical symptoms like fatigue, frequent headaches, or difficulty sleeping, as well as emotional symptoms like irritability or lack of motivation. These can be signs that your current balance is skewed.
4. Diminished Productivity Evaluate whether your productivity at work is declining. Difficulty focusing, procrastination, and reduced performance can all be consequences of an imbalance between work and personal life.

Practical Tip: Your body often gives the earliest clues about imbalance. If you notice frequent headaches, fatigue, or irritability, take these signs seriously. Schedule short breaks throughout your day to check in on how you're feeling physically and emotionally. This simple practice can help you catch potential imbalances early before they turn into bigger issues.

Setting Personal Goals

With a clear understanding of your current balance and identified imbalances, the next step is to set realistic and actionable goals.

Effective goal setting involves:

1. Specificity Define specific areas you want to address. For example, if you identify a lack of personal time, set a goal to allocate specific hours each week for personal activities or family time.
2. Measurability Ensure your goals are measurable. For instance, you might aim to reduce overtime by 10 hours per week or increase family time by 5 hours each week.
3. Achievability Set goals that are achievable within your current circumstances. If you are working long hours due to a tight project deadline, set incremental goals to gradually restore balance once the project is completed.
4. Time-Bound Create a timeline for achieving your goals. Short-term goals might be weekly or monthly, while long-term goals could extend over several months or a year. Regularly review your progress and adjust as needed.
5. Action Plan Develop an action plan outlining steps to achieve your goals. For example, if improving personal time is a goal, your action plan might include scheduling regular family activities, setting boundaries for work hours, and exploring flexible work arrangements if possible.

By systematically assessing your current balance, identifying imbalances, and setting actionable goals, you will be better equipped to make meaningful changes that enhance both your professional effectiveness and personal fulfillment.

Practical Tip: Choose one specific area you want to improve and set a small, realistic goal around it. For example, if personal time is lacking, aim to set aside just 30 minutes a day for a hobby or relaxation. This small win can build momentum and make larger changes feel more manageable. Breaking down your goals into simple, actionable steps makes it easier to stay committed and see progress.

CHAPTER 3: TIME MANAGEMENT TECHNIQUES

Effective time management is crucial for creating a harmonious balance between work and personal life. It allows you to allocate your time wisely, ensuring that you not only meet your professional obligations but also carve out space for personal fulfillment and relaxation. By mastering the art of prioritization, you can focus on high-impact tasks first, preventing the overwhelm that comes from trying to juggle everything at once. Techniques such as the Pomodoro Technique offer structured intervals of focused work, which can boost productivity while allowing for regular breaks, thereby reducing burnout.

In addition to these strategies, leveraging modern tools and apps can further streamline your workflow. From digital planners and task managers to time-tracking apps, these resources can help you stay organized, track your progress, and adjust your approach as needed. By integrating these time management techniques into your routine, you'll not only enhance your efficiency but also foster a more balanced and less stressful lifestyle.

Prioritization and Planning

◆ ◆ ◆

Prioritizing tasks and planning your day are foundational to effective time management. By focusing on what matters most and organizing your schedule accordingly, you can ensure that you address critical tasks first and manage your workload more efficiently.

1. The Eisenhower Matrix

The Eisenhower Matrix is a powerful tool for prioritizing tasks based on their urgency and importance. It divides tasks into four categories:

- Urgent and Important: Tasks that require immediate attention and contribute to significant outcomes (e.g., meeting deadlines, addressing crises).
- Important but Not Urgent: Tasks that are crucial for long-term goals but don't need immediate action (e.g., strategic planning, skill development).
- Urgent but Not Important: Tasks that require prompt action but don't contribute significantly to your long-term goals (e.g., interruptions, minor requests).
- Neither Urgent nor Important: Tasks that are neither pressing nor valuable (e.g., trivial activities, excessive social media).

How to Use It:

- List your tasks and categorize them into four quadrants.
- Focus on completing tasks in the "Urgent and Important" quadrant first.
- Delegate or minimize tasks in the "Urgent but Not Important" and "Neither Urgent nor Important" quadrants.

Practical Tip: At the beginning of each week, list out your tasks and categorize them based on urgency and importance. Focus on completing high-priority tasks first and allocate specific time blocks for them in your schedule.

2. The ABCDE Method

The ABCDE Method helps you prioritize tasks by assigning them letters based on their importance:

A: Must-do tasks with serious consequences if not completed (e.g., project deadlines).

B: Should-do tasks with minor consequences (e.g., attending meetings).

C: Nice-to-do tasks with no significant consequences (e.g., organizing files).

D: Delegate tasks that others can handle (e.g., administrative tasks).

E: Eliminate tasks that are unnecessary (e.g., redundant paperwork).

How to Use It:

- List all your tasks.
- Assign each task a letter based on its importance.
- Focus on "A" tasks first and delegate or eliminate lower-priority tasks.

Practical Tip: Use a planner or digital calendar to map out your tasks, deadlines, and appointments. Break larger projects into smaller, manageable steps and set deadlines for each step to maintain steady progress.

The Pomodoro Technique and Beyond

The Pomodoro Technique is a well-known time management

method that boosts focus and productivity by dividing work into short, manageable intervals. Learn how this technique, along with other time management strategies, can help you stay concentrated, prevent burnout, and improve overall efficiency.

1. The Pomodoro Technique

The Pomodoro Technique involves working in focused intervals, typically 25 minutes, followed by a 5-minute break. After four intervals, take a longer break of 15-30 minutes. This technique helps maintain concentration and prevents burnout.

How to Use It:

- Choose a task to work on.
- Set a timer for 25 minutes and work on the task until the timer goes off.
- Take a 5-minute break.
- After four intervals, take a longer break.

Practical Tip: Use a timer or a Pomodoro app to track your work intervals and breaks. Adjust the length of work and break periods based on your personal productivity and focus levels.

2. Time Blocking

Time blocking involves scheduling specific blocks of time for different tasks or activities throughout your day. This approach helps you allocate dedicated time for both work and personal activities, reducing the likelihood of multitasking and distractions.

How to Use It:

- Identify the key activities you need to accomplish (e.g., project work, meetings, exercise).
- Block out specific times in your calendar for each activity.

- Stick to your schedule as closely as possible and adjust as needed.

Practical Tip: Choose a single day to experiment with time blocking. Allocate distinct time slots for work tasks, personal activities, and breaks. This focused approach helps you see how well it works in practice and allows you to fine-tune your schedule for better efficiency and balance.

3. The 2-Minute Rule

The 2-Minute Rule, popularized by productivity expert David Allen, suggests that if a task can be completed in 2 minutes or less, do it immediately rather than postponing it. This helps prevent small tasks from piling up and becoming overwhelming.

How to Use It:

- Identify tasks that take 2 minutes or less (e.g., responding to quick emails, or making a phone call).
- Complete these tasks right away to keep your to-do list manageable.

Practical Tip: Whenever you encounter a task that will take 2 minutes or less, tackle it immediately. This quick action keeps your to-do list from becoming cluttered and helps you maintain momentum throughout the day.

Tools and Apps for Better Time Management

Utilizing modern tools and apps can streamline your time management efforts, making it easier to stay organized and productive. From task trackers to calendar apps, these tools offer a variety of features to support efficient time management.

- ❖ Task Management Tools
    - · Trello: Organize tasks into boards and lists, and track progress visually.
    - · Asana: Manage projects and tasks, assign deadlines, and collaborate with teams.
- ❖ Calendar Apps
    - · Google Calendar: Schedule events, set reminders, and view your daily, weekly, or monthly agenda.
    - · Outlook Calendar: Integrate with email and set appointments, meetings, and deadlines.
- ❖ Focus and Productivity Apps
    - · Focus@Will: Provides background music designed to enhance concentration.
    - · Forest: Helps you stay focused by growing a virtual tree as you work uninterrupted.
- ❖ Time Tracking Tools
    - · Toggl: Track the time you spend on various tasks and projects.
    - · Clockify: Provides insight into how your time is spent and helps you manage productivity.

Practical Tip: Pick one tool from the categories listed, whether it's a task manager like Trello, a calendar app like Google Calendar, or a time tracker like Toggl, and integrate it into your routine for a week. This focused trial will help you see its impact on your productivity and organization without overwhelming you with multiple new tools at once.

Implementing Time Management Techniques

Successfully integrating time management techniques into your daily life requires a strategic approach. It's not enough to merely understand these techniques; you must actively apply them to see tangible improvements in productivity and work-life balance. This section provides actionable steps to implement these techniques effectively, helping you to streamline your tasks and maximize your efficiency.

To successfully implement these time management techniques, start by:

- Identifying Your Priorities: Use prioritization methods to determine which tasks and activities are most important.
- Creating a Structured Schedule: Apply time-blocking strategies to allocate dedicated time for each task.
- Leveraging Technology: Utilize tools and apps to organize and track your tasks and time effectively.
- Regular Review and Adjustment: Periodically review your schedule and adjust as needed to accommodate changes in priorities or workload.

Practical Tip: At the end of each week or month, review your progress and assess the effectiveness of your time management strategies. Adjust as needed to address any challenges and refine your approach for continued success.

By prioritizing tasks and utilizing planning methods, implementing strategies like the Pomodoro Technique, and leveraging modern tools and apps, you can optimize your workflow, reduce stress, and maintain a harmonious balanced, and fulfilling life.

CHAPTER 4: SETTING BOUNDARIES

Creating and maintaining boundaries is essential for achieving a balanced and fulfilling life. Boundaries serve as crucial safeguards for your time and well-being, helping to manage the demands of work while preserving space for personal activities and relaxation. By setting clear work hours and defining distinct personal zones, you can reduce stress and prevent burnout, allowing you to be more present and engaged in all areas of your life.

Understanding the significance of a "no work zone" and learning how to communicate your boundaries effectively are key components of this process. Establishing these limits helps create a clear separation between professional responsibilities and personal time, fostering a healthier work-life balance. This section delves into practical strategies for setting and maintaining these boundaries, ensuring that you can protect your time and enjoy a more harmonious lifestyle.

Establishing Clear Work Hours

◆ ◆ ◆

Creating a well-defined schedule is a cornerstone of effective boundary-setting. By establishing clear work hours, you set specific times for professional tasks, allowing you to separate work from personal time. This practice not only helps manage your workload but also reinforces a structure that supports a healthier work-life balance.

1. Defining Your Work Hours

The first step in setting boundaries is defining your work hours. Clearly outline when you will be available for work-related tasks and when you will be off duty. This not only helps you manage your own time but also sets expectations for others.

How to Define Your Work Hours:

- Assess Your Needs: Consider your job requirements and personal preferences. Determine the core hours during which you are most productive and can handle work tasks efficiently.
- Set Specific Times: Specify start and end times for your workday. For example, you might choose to work from 9:00 AM to 5:00 PM, Monday through Friday.
- Account for Flexibility: If your job allows flexibility, define a range within which you will work. This could be 8:00 AM to 6:00 PM with the flexibility to start or end your day earlier or later.

Practical Tip: Create a work schedule that fits your productivity peaks and personal commitments. Stick to this schedule as closely as possible to build a routine and maintain a clear separation between work and personal time.

2. Creating a Routine

Once you have established your work hours, create a daily routine that aligns with them. Consistency in your routine can help reinforce your boundaries and reduce the likelihood of work spilling into personal time.

How to Create a Routine:

- Start and End Rituals: Develop rituals to signal the beginning and end of your workday. This might include a morning routine such as making coffee or an evening routine like shutting down your computer.
- Scheduled Breaks: Incorporate regular breaks into your routine to avoid burnout and maintain productivity. Schedule short breaks throughout the day and a longer lunch break.
- Transition Time: Allocate a brief period to transition from work mode to personal mode. This can help you mentally shift gears and prepare for personal activities.

Practical Tip: Implement a simple ritual to signal the end of your workday, such as a five-minute walk or a quick evening stretch. This helps create a clear boundary between work and personal time, making it easier to switch off and enjoy your time away from work.

The Importance of a "No Work Zone"

A designated "no work zone" is essential for preserving your personal space and downtime. By creating areas in your home or office where work is off-limits, you foster environments that encourage relaxation and rejuvenation, helping to prevent work from overwhelming your personal life.

1. Defining Your "No Work Zone"

Creating a physical and mental "no work zone" is essential for maintaining a clear boundary between work and personal life. This space should be free from work-related distractions and should promote relaxation and personal activities.

How to Define Your "No Work Zone":

- Choose a Designated Space: If you work from home, select a specific area for work and keep it separate from spaces associated with relaxation or family time. For example, avoid setting up a home office in your bedroom or dining area.
- Set Up Clear Boundaries: Make it a rule that work materials and electronic devices used for work are not brought into your "no work zone." This helps to physically and mentally separate work from personal life.

Practical Tip: Establish rules for your "no work zones," such as no work-related conversations or devices allowed. Make these areas comfortable and conducive to relaxation and personal activities.

3. The Psychological Impact

The psychological benefits of maintaining a "no work zone" include reduced stress and improved mental clarity. By creating a distinct boundary, you signal to yourself and others that this space is reserved for personal time and relaxation.

How to Benefit Psychologically:

- Relaxation and Recovery: Use your "no work zone" to engage in activities that help you unwind, such as reading, hobbies, or spending time with loved ones.
- Improved Focus: Knowing you have a dedicated work area can help you concentrate better during work hours, leading to increased productivity and job satisfaction.

Practical Tip: To fully benefit from your 'no work zone,' create a simple ritual that signals the transition from work mode to relaxation mode. This could be as straightforward as changing into comfortable clothes, lighting a candle, or playing calming music. By consistently practicing this ritual, you reinforce the mental boundary between work and personal time, helping your mind to relax and recover more effectively.

Communicating Boundaries Effectively

◆ ◆ ◆

Clear and assertive communication is key to ensuring that your boundaries are respected. By effectively articulating your limits to colleagues, clients, and family members, you establish mutual understanding and prevent potential conflicts, creating a balanced and harmonious work environment.

1. Setting Expectations with Colleagues

Communicating your boundaries to colleagues is essential for ensuring that your work hours and personal time are respected. Clear communication helps prevent misunderstandings and promotes a healthy work environment.

How to Communicate Boundaries:

- Be Clear and Direct: Clearly articulate your work hours and availability to your colleagues. Let them know when you are and aren't available for meetings or communications.
- Use Tools and Signals: Utilize tools such as email autoreplies or status indicators on communication platforms to inform others of your availability.

Practical Tip: Use tools such as automated email responses or calendar invites to communicate your availability. Clearly state your working hours and times when you are not available for work-related matters.

2. Balancing Family and Personal Boundaries

Balancing work boundaries with family and personal time requires open communication and mutual understanding. Share your work schedule with family members and discuss how they can support your boundaries.

How to Balance Family and Personal Boundaries:

- Schedule Family Time: Set specific times for family activities and ensure they are prioritized in your schedule. This demonstrates your commitment to personal relationships and helps maintain work-life harmony.
- Discuss Expectations: Have conversations with family members about your work hours and the importance of uninterrupted work time. Encourage them to respect these boundaries while also being flexible when necessary.

Practical Tip: Set aside time each week to discuss your work schedule and any upcoming family activities. This proactive approach helps align expectations, ensures family time is prioritized, and reinforces mutual support for maintaining your work-life balance.

3. Handling Boundary Violations

Ocasionally, there may be situations where boundaries are challenged. It's important to address these situations calmly and assertively to maintain your balance.

How to Handle Violations:

- Address Issues Promptly: If a colleague or family member oversteps your boundaries, address the issue as soon as possible. Communicate your concerns clearly and propose solutions.

- Reinforce Your Boundaries: Remind others of your established boundaries as needed and reaffirm your commitment to maintaining them.

Practical Tip: If your boundaries are tested, calmly and assertively remind others of your limits. Reinforce your boundaries as needed while maintaining a professional and respectful demeanor.

By establishing clear work hours, creating a "no work zone," and effectively communicating your boundaries, you can foster a more balanced and fulfilling work-life dynamic. These practices help protect your time, reduce stress, and enhance both professional and personal satisfaction.

CHAPTER 5: MANAGING STRESS AND AVOIDING BURNOUT

Achieving work-life balance hinges significantly on your ability to manage stress and prevent burnout. When left unchecked, stress and burnout can undermine your health, erode your productivity, and diminish your overall satisfaction with both work and life. Recognizing the early signs of stress and burnout is the first step towards mitigating their effects. This section will guide you through identifying these warning signs, introduce practical techniques for reducing stress, and offer strategies to cultivate a resilient mindset. By addressing these areas, you'll be better equipped to maintain your well-being and sustain a balanced, fulfilling life.

Recognizing the Signs of Stress and Burnout

Recognizing the early warning signs of stress and burnout is essential for preserving a healthy work-life balance. By spotting these indicators early, you can take proactive measures to address them before they escalate. This will guide you in identifying both subtle and obvious signs of stress and burnout, allowing you to seek appropriate help and apply strategies to safeguard your well-being.

1. Identifying Stress Symptoms

Stress manifests in various ways, both physically and emotionally. Recognizing these symptoms early can help you address them before they escalate into more severe issues.

Physical Symptoms:

- Chronic Fatigue: Persistent tiredness despite adequate rest.
- Headaches: Frequent tension or migraine headaches.
- Gastrointestinal: Problems such as stomachaches, constipation, or diarrhea.
- Sleep Disturbances: Difficulty falling or staying asleep or experiencing restless sleep.
- Muscle Tension: Pain in the shoulders, neck, or back.

Practical Tip: Pay attention to any persistent physical symptoms and assess whether they correlate with increased stress or overwork. Regular check-ups with a healthcare provider can help monitor and address these symptoms.

Emotional Symptoms:

- Irritability: Increased frustration or mood swings.
- Anxiety: Persistent worry or a sense of impending doom.
- Lack of Motivation: Reduced interest in tasks or a sense of apathy.
- Overwhelm: Feeling swamped by responsibilities or unable to cope.
- Depression: Decrease in appetite, sense of withdrawal, loneliness.

Practical Tip: Monitor your emotional state and mental well-being. Journaling or using mindfulness practices can help track your feelings and identify patterns related to stress.

2. Recognizing Burnout

Burnout is a more severe state of chronic stress characterized by emotional exhaustion, depersonalization, and a reduced sense of accomplishment. It typically occurs over an extended period and can severely impact your personal and professional life.

Signs of Burnout:

- Emotional Exhaustion: Feeling drained, fatigued, and emotionally depleted.
- Cynicism: Developing a negative, detached attitude towards work or people.
- Decreased Performance: Struggling to maintain productivity or meet expectations.
- Detachment: Feeling disconnected from work or personal relationships.

Practical Tip: Reflect on any changes in your behavior, such as procrastination or avoiding social activities. Recognizing these changes early can help you address the root causes before they lead to more serious issues.

Stress Reduction Techniques

Implementing effective stress reduction techniques can help manage daily pressures and prevent burnout. Incorporating these practices into your routine can improve your overall well-being and enhance your ability to handle stress.

1. Mindfulness and Meditation

Mindfulness and meditation techniques are effective in soothing the mind and alleviating stress. They focus on bringing your attention to the present moment and fostering a non-judgmental awareness of your thoughts and emotions.

Mindfulness Techniques:

- Mindful Breathing: Focus on your breath, inhaling deeply and exhaling slowly. This can help center your mind and reduce anxiety.
- Body Scan Meditation: Pay attention to different parts of your body, noticing any tension or discomfort, and consciously relax those areas.
- Meditation Practices:
- Guided Meditation: Use guided meditation apps or recordings that lead you through relaxation exercises and visualizations.
- Loving-Kindness Meditation: Practice sending positive thoughts and well-wishes to yourself and others, fostering compassion and emotional resilience.

Practical Tip: Set aside a few minutes each day for mindfulness or meditation. Use apps or guided sessions to help you establish regular practice and integrate it into your daily routine.

2. Physical Activity

Regular physical activity is a powerful stress reliever. Exercise releases endorphins, which improve mood and reduce feelings of stress.

Effective Activities:

- Aerobic Exercise: Engage in activities such as walking, jogging, or cycling to boost cardiovascular health and reduce stress.
- Strength Training: Incorporate weightlifting or resistance exercises to build physical strength and mental resilience.

- Yoga: Practice yoga to combine physical movement with mindfulness, improving flexibility and promoting relaxation.

Practical Tip: Incorporate at least 30 minutes of physical activity into your daily routine. Choose activities you enjoy, such as walking, swimming, or yoga, to make exercise a sustainable and enjoyable part of your life.

3. Time Management

Effective time management alleviates stress by enabling you to organize your tasks and allocate your time more efficiently. This approach helps you avoid the pressure and anxiety of last-minute rushes, ensuring that you complete tasks on time and maintain a smoother, more controlled workflow.

Time Management Strategies:
- Prioritize Tasks: Use prioritization techniques to focus on the most important tasks first.
- Delegate: Assign tasks to others, when possible, to reduce your workload.
- Set Realistic Goals: Break larger tasks into manageable steps and set achievable deadlines.

Practical Tip: Schedule a 10-minute planning session at the start of each day to prioritize tasks, delegate when possible, and set realistic goals. This brief, focused session can help you organize your day efficiently, reduce stress, and prevent last-minute rushes.

Creating a Resilient Mindset

Developing a resilient mindset is essential for effectively managing stress and avoiding burnout. Resilience helps you navigate challenges, adapt to change, and maintain a positive outlook despite difficulties.

1. Cultivate a Growth Mindset

A growth mindset is the belief that abilities and intelligence can be developed through effort and learning. Cultivating this mindset helps you view challenges as opportunities for growth rather than insurmountable obstacles.

How to Develop a Growth Mindset:

- Embrace Challenges: Approach difficulties with curiosity and a willingness to learn.
- Learn from Criticism: Use feedback as a tool for improvement rather than taking it personally.
- Celebrate Effort: Focus on the effort and progress made, rather than just the outcome.

Practical Tip: When receiving feedback, view it as a valuable opportunity for learning and improvement. Instead of focusing on any negative aspects, analyze how the feedback can help you grow and apply it to enhance your skills and abilities.

2. Building Emotional Resilience

Emotional resilience involves adapting to adversity and bouncing back from setbacks. Strengthening your emotional resilience can help you manage stress more effectively and maintain a positive outlook. Reach out for support when needed and offer support in return to create a mutually beneficial network.

Strategies for Building Resilience:

- Cultivate Positive Relationships: Invest in building

and maintaining supportive relationships with friends, family, and colleagues.

- Practice Self-Care: Self-care is essential for maintaining resilience and managing stress effectively. Prioritize activities that nurture your physical, emotional, and mental well-being.
- Develop Problem-Solving Skills: Reframe challenges as opportunities to develop new skills or gain valuable experience. Focus on what you can learn from each situation rather than dwelling on setbacks.

Practical Tip: Regularly connect with friends, family, and colleagues to build a strong support system. Share your challenges and offer support in return, creating a network that enhances your emotional resilience and helps you navigate stress more effectively.

2. Setting Realistic Expectations

Setting achievable goals and expectations helps prevent overwhelm and burnout. Recognize your limits and avoid overcommitting.

How to Set Realistic Expectations:

- Assess Your Capacity: Be honest about how much you can handle and adjust your commitments accordingly.
- Communicate Clearly: Set clear expectations with others regarding your availability and workload.
- Adjust as Needed: Regularly review and adjust your goals and commitments based on your current situation and capacity.

Practical Tip: Regularly evaluate your workload and be transparent with others about what you can realistically handle.

By setting clear boundaries and adjusting your commitments based on your current capacity, you can prevent overwhelm and maintain a manageable workload.

By recognizing the signs of stress and burnout, implementing stress reduction techniques, and fostering a resilient mindset, you can enhance your ability to navigate challenges and sustain well-being. Incorporate these strategies into your daily routine to build resilience, improve your overall health, and create a more harmonious work-life balance.

CHAPTER 6: BUILDING SUPPORT SYSTEMS

Developing a strong support system is crucial for maintaining a healthy work-life balance. Such a system offers vital emotional, practical, and professional support, which can significantly ease the challenges of managing work and personal responsibilities. By effectively utilizing the support of family and friends, seeking professional help when necessary, and fostering a positive work environment, you create a network that enhances your ability to navigate difficulties and sustain your overall well-being. This section delves into strategies for building and leveraging these support networks to strengthen your balance and resilience.

Leveraging Family and Friends

Your support network plays a pivotal role in achieving work-life balance. Leveraging the support of family and friends can provide emotional encouragement, practical assistance, and a sense of connection. This section explores how to effectively tap into your personal network to enhance your well-being and navigate the demands of both work and life.

1. Communicating Your Needs

Your family and friends can be valuable allies in your pursuit of work-life balance. Open communication about your needs and challenges allows them to provide the appropriate support.

How to Communicate Effectively:

- Be Honest and Specific: Share your current struggles and what kind of support would be most helpful. For example, you might explain that you need more help with household chores or emotional support during stressful periods.
- Set Clear Boundaries: Discuss your work schedule and personal time with your loved ones to ensure they understand when you need uninterrupted time for work and when you are available for family activities.
- Request Help Proactively: If you need assistance, don't hesitate to ask for it directly. Whether it's help with childcare, a listening ear, or practical support, being clear about your needs can lead to better outcomes.

Practical Tip: Clearly communicate your needs to family and friends by explaining exactly what support you require, such as help with household tasks or emotional backing during busy times. By setting clear boundaries and asking for help proactively, you ensure that your loved ones understand how they can best support you.

2. Fostering Mutual Support

A balanced support system involves both giving and receiving help. Building strong, reciprocal relationships ensures that support is mutual and sustainable.

How to Foster Mutual Support:

- Offer Support in Return: Be available to support your family and friends when they need it. This reciprocal approach strengthens relationships and creates a network of mutual assistance.
- Celebrate Achievements Together: Share successes and

milestones with your loved ones, acknowledging their role in your journey and fostering a sense of shared accomplishment.

Practical Tip: Schedule regular check-ins with family and friends to discuss your current priorities and challenges. Being transparent about your needs helps others understand how they can best support you.

Your support network is essential for achieving work-life balance, providing emotional support, practical help, and a sense of connection. To make the most of this network, communicate your needs clearly and openly with family and friends. Be specific about the kind of support you need, set clear boundaries to distinguish work from personal time, and ask for help proactively.

Additionally, fostering mutual support by offering assistance in return and celebrating achievements together strengthens these relationships. Regular check-ins with your support network can ensure ongoing, reciprocal support that enhances your well-being and helps you manage the demands of both work and life effectively.

Seeking Professional Help When Needed

Sometimes, managing work-life balance requires more than self-help strategies and support from family and friends. Seeking professional help can provide valuable insights, coping strategies, and tailored solutions to address complex challenges. Consulting experts such as counselors, coaches, or therapists and how their support can enhance your ability to maintain balance and achieve your goals.

1. Understanding the Benefits of Professional Support

Sometimes, managing work-life balance requires more specialized assistance. Seeking professional help can provide valuable insights, strategies, and support tailored to your specific needs. Early intervention can prevent issues from escalating.

Types of Professional Help:

- Counselors and Therapists: Mental health professionals can help you address stress, anxiety, or other emotional challenges. They offer strategies for coping, problem-solving, and improving mental well-being.
- Coaches: Life or career coaches can provide guidance on achieving personal and professional goals, managing time effectively, and improving work-life balance.
- Financial Advisors: If financial stress is impacting your balance, a financial advisor can help you develop strategies for budgeting, saving, and managing financial responsibilities.

Practical Tip: If you're struggling with work-life balance, consider reaching out to a counselor, coach, or financial advisor for specialized support. Early intervention with these professionals can provide tailored strategies and insights, helping you address issues before they escalate and improve your overall well-being.

2. Finding the Right Professional

Selecting a professional who meets your needs involves understanding their expertise and approach. Research and consider recommendations to find someone who aligns with your goals. Selecting the appropriate professional is crucial for effective support.

How to Find the Right Fit:

- Check Qualifications: Ensure the professional has relevant credentials and experience in their field.
- Seek Recommendations: Ask for referrals from trusted sources or read reviews to gauge the professional's reputation and effectiveness.
- Schedule a Consultation: Many professionals offer initial consultations to discuss your needs and determine if they are a good fit for you.
- Celebrate Achievements Together: Share successes and milestones with your loved ones, acknowledging their role in your journey and fostering a sense of shared accomplishment.

Practical Tip: When selecting a professional for support, verify their qualifications and seek recommendations from trusted sources. Take advantage of initial consultations to discuss your needs and assess if their approach aligns with your goals, ensuring you choose the right fit for effective assistance.

3. Utilize Professional Resources

Make use of the resources and tools provided by professionals. These may include coping strategies, goal-setting techniques, or stress management plans that can enhance your ability to achieve balance.

Examples of resources and tools:

- Implement Coping Strategies: Actively apply the coping strategies recommended by your professional. This might include techniques such as mindfulness, cognitive-behavioral exercises, or time management practices designed to help manage stress and improve your overall well-being.

- Set and Track Goals: Use the goal-setting techniques provided by your professional to establish clear, actionable objectives. Regularly review and track your progress towards these goals, adjusting your strategies as needed based on feedback and results.
- Follow Up and Adjust: Schedule follow-up sessions to discuss your progress with your professional. Address any challenges or concerns you encounter and be open to modifying the strategies or plans to better suit your evolving needs and circumstances.

Practical Tip: Leverage the tools and strategies offered by professionals to enhance your work-life balance. Implement recommended coping techniques, set and track your goals using their methods, and schedule regular follow-ups to discuss your progress. This proactive approach helps you stay on course, address challenges effectively, and adjust your plans as needed.

4. Overcoming Stigma and Barriers

Seeking help is a proactive step towards well-being and should be viewed positively. Overcoming any stigma or reluctance about seeking professional assistance can be empowering and beneficial.

How to Overcome Barriers:
- Acknowledge the Benefits: Recognize that seeking help is a sign of strength and a commitment to improving your quality of life.
- Normalize the Process: Understand that many people seek professional help and that it is a common and accepted practice for addressing challenges.
- Address Financial Concerns: Explore options such as insurance coverage or sliding-scale fees to make professional help more accessible.

Practical Tip: View seeking professional help as a proactive and empowering step towards improving your well-being. Embrace the process by acknowledging its benefits, normalizing it as a common practice, and exploring financial options like insurance or sliding-scale fees to reduce barriers.

Building a Supportive Work Environment

Creating a nurturing work environment is key to balancing professional success and personal well-being. Foster collaboration, open communication, and mutual respect, transforming your workplace into a source of encouragement and growth. Discover strategies to connect with colleagues, build trust, and advocate for a culture that supports everyone's journey toward work-life harmony.

1. Cultivating Positive Relationships at Work

A supportive work environment can significantly impact your work-life balance and overall job satisfaction. Building positive relationships with colleagues and supervisors creates a collaborative and understanding workplace.

How to Cultivate Positive Relationships:

- Foster Open Communication: Encourage transparent communication with your colleagues and supervisors. Share your work preferences, challenges, and any support you may need.
- Show Appreciation: Recognize and appreciate the efforts of others. Acknowledging the contributions of your colleagues fosters a positive and supportive atmosphere.
- Participate in Team Building: Engage in team-building activities and social events to strengthen relationships

and build camaraderie.

Practical Tip: Enhance your work environment by fostering open communication with colleagues and supervisors, showing appreciation for their efforts, and actively participating in team-building activities. These practices help create a collaborative and supportive workplace, improving your overall job satisfaction and work-life balance.

2. Establishing Work-Life Balance Policies

Workplaces that support work-life balance often have policies in place to promote flexibility and well-being. Advocating for or taking advantage of these policies can help create a more balanced work environment.

Key Policies to Consider:

- Flexible Work Arrangements: Policies that allow for flexible hours, remote work, or compressed workweeks can help employees manage their personal and professional responsibilities more effectively.
- Employee Assistance Programs (EAPs): EAPs provide confidential counseling and support services to help employees deal with personal and work-related issues.

Wellness Programs: Programs that promote health and well-being, such as fitness incentives or stress management workshops, contribute to a supportive work environment.

Practical Tip: Advocate for or utilize existing work-life balance policies at your workplace, such as flexible work arrangements, Employee Assistance Programs (EAPs), and wellness programs. These resources can help you manage personal and professional responsibilities more effectively, contributing to a healthier work environment and better overall balance.

3. Seeking Support from HR and Management

If you encounter challenges related to work-life balance, reaching out to Human Resources (HR) or management can be an effective way to find solutions and support.

How to Seek Support:

- Discuss Your Concerns: Share any work-related challenges or needs with HR or your manager. They may offer solutions or adjustments to help you achieve better balance.
- Provide Feedback: Offer constructive feedback on work policies and practices that could be improved to better support employees' work-life balance.

Practical Tip: If you face work-life balance challenges, proactively discuss your concerns with HR or your manager. Clearly communicate any difficulties you're experiencing and provide constructive feedback on how work policies could be improved. This dialogue can lead to practical adjustments and better support.

By leveraging the support of family and friends, seeking professional help when needed, and building a supportive work environment, you create a strong network that enhances your ability to achieve and maintain a balanced life. This holistic approach ensures that you have the resources and assistance necessary to thrive both personally and professionally.

CHAPTER 7: EMBRACING FLEXIBILITY AND ADAPTATION

Modern life is a constant balancing act, where we are often tasked with managing various personal, professional, and social responsibilities simultaneously. This dynamic environment makes flexibility not just a convenience but a crucial factor in achieving a true work-life balance. Gone are the days when rigid routines and strict boundaries define success and productivity. In today's fast-paced world, holding on too tightly to fixed schedules can lead to undue stress, burnout, and a sense of inadequacy when things inevitably don't go as planned.

Being flexible is about more than just adjusting to changes — it's about understanding that balance is a fluid concept. What works one day may not work the next, and that's perfectly okay. This mindset shift can relieve a lot of pressure, allowing you to adapt to life's ebbs and flows with greater ease. Whether it's dealing with unexpected meetings, family obligations, or self-care needs, embracing flexibility means recognizing that work-life balance is not static; it continually evolves as your priorities, responsibilities, and circumstances change.

In this chapter, we'll delve deeper into the significance of adopting a flexible mindset. We will explore practical strategies to navigate change, such as how to set realistic goals, reprioritize tasks, and manage time effectively when things don't go according to plan.

We'll also examine the benefits and challenges of remote work and flexible hours, offering tips on how to maximize productivity while maintaining personal well-being. By the end of this chapter, you'll have a clearer understanding of how flexibility can be a powerful tool in creating a balanced, fulfilling life.

The Role of Flexibility in Work-Life Balance

Flexibility is the foundation of a balanced life. It involves being able to adjust plans, shift priorities, and respond to unexpected events without feeling overwhelmed. A flexible approach allows you to meet the demands of work while also tending to personal needs. For example, some days might require extra work hours to meet a deadline, while others may offer an opportunity to focus on self-care or family time. The ability to adapt to these variations helps reduce stress and prevents the feeling of being stretched too thin. Flexibility enhances work-life balance through Enhancing Resilience and Improving Time Management.

1. Enhancing Resilience

Flexibility fosters resilience by enabling you to adapt to new situations and recover from setbacks. When you are flexible, you can manage stress more effectively and maintain a positive outlook even when faced with disruptions to your routine.

Here are some examples of how flexibility fosters resilience:

- Navigating Changes in the Work Environment:
    - Scenario: Your workplace undergoes significant

changes, such as a new management structure or remote transition.

- ◦ Flexible Response: You embrace the changes by learning new tools, adjusting your work habits, and seeking support from colleagues. You stay open to feedback and adapt your approach based on the evolving environment.
- ◦ Resilience Outcome: Your ability to adapt to the new work environment helps you manage stress and maintain productivity, as you view the change as an opportunity to develop new skills.
- Managing Shifts in Personal Goals:
  - ◦ Scenario: Your personal goals or priorities shift due to changing circumstances, such as a new hobby or family obligation.
  - ◦ Flexible Response: You adjust your daily routine and long-term plans to incorporate these new priorities. This might involve reallocating time for personal development or adjusting your work schedule to align with your new goals.
  - ◦ Resilience Outcome: By adapting to changing personal goals, you maintain a balanced life and reduce stress, ensuring that you continue to grow and stay positive despite the shifts in priorities.

Practical Tip: Develop a flexible mindset by treating challenges as opportunities for growth. Reframe setbacks as learning experiences and focus on the positive aspects of change.

2. Improving Time Management

Being flexible allows you to adjust your time management strategies to accommodate evolving demands. Instead of adhering rigidly to a predetermined schedule, flexibility enables you to prioritize tasks based on current needs and adjust deadlines as necessary.

Here are examples of how improving time management through flexibility can help you accommodate evolving demands:

- Reprioritizing Tasks During Peak Work Periods:
  - Scenario: You face an influx of urgent tasks and requests during a particularly busy period.
  - Flexible Response: You quickly identify the most critical tasks and focus on completing them first. You temporarily delay or delegate less urgent tasks and use time blocks to handle the increased workload efficiently.
  - Outcome: Flexibility in prioritizing tasks helps you manage peak work periods without becoming overwhelmed, ensuring that the most important tasks are completed on time.
- Handling Changes in Personal Responsibilities:
  - Scenario: A family event or personal obligation arises, requiring you to shift your work schedule.
  - Flexible Response: You adjust your work hours or redistribute tasks to fit around your personal commitment. You communicate with your team about the changes and use flexible work arrangements to balance both personal and professional demands.
  - Outcome: Flexibility in managing your schedule allows you to fulfill personal responsibilities while ensuring that work tasks are still completed, achieving a balanced and effective approach.

Practical Tip: Design a flexible schedule with buffer times for unexpected tasks or changes. Regularly review and adjust your plan to reflect shifting priorities and deadlines.

Flexibility is crucial for maintaining a balanced life, as it allows you to adapt to changes and manage both work and personal demands without becoming overwhelmed. Being flexible enhances resilience by helping you handle disruptions and stress more effectively. It also improves time management by enabling you to adjust your schedule and priorities based on current needs. To embrace flexibility, treat challenges as growth opportunities and create a flexible schedule with buffer times for unexpected changes. Regularly review and adjust your plans to stay aligned with shifting priorities and deadlines.

Strategies for Adapting to Change

Change is an inevitable part of life. Whether it's an unexpected project at work, a shift in personal commitments, or global events that disrupt our daily routines, the ability to adapt is crucial.

Here are some strategies to help you embrace change and maintain balance:

1. Reframe Your Perspective: Instead of viewing change as a disruption, try to see it as an opportunity for growth. Shifting your mindset can reduce resistance and make it easier to find new ways to balance your responsibilities. Look for positives in the situation—new skills you can learn or ways the change might simplify other aspects of your life.

2. Set Flexible Goals: While having clear goals is important, it's equally important to allow some flexibility in how and when you achieve them. Setting goals with a built-in buffer or contingency plan helps you adapt when unexpected changes arise. For example, if you're working toward a professional milestone, set smaller,

more manageable steps that can be adjusted as needed.

3. Prioritize Self-Care During Transitions: Change, even positive change, can be stressful. Make sure to prioritize self-care during times of transition. Incorporate activities that help you relax and recharge, whether it's exercise, meditation, or spending time with loved ones. Taking care of your mental and physical well-being will enhance your ability to adapt effectively.

4. Communicate Your Needs: Open communication is key when navigating changes in both personal and professional settings. Share your needs, concerns, and limitations with colleagues, family members, or friends. Being clear about what you need helps build understanding and support, making it easier to adapt to new situations.

5. Stay Organized but Flexible: Planning is helpful, but plans don't always go as expected. Use tools like to- do lists or scheduling apps to keep track of your commitments but be prepared to rearrange tasks as priorities shift. Having a structured yet flexible approach can reduce the feeling of chaos when things don't go according to plan.

Practical Tip: Embrace Change by adopting a flexible mindset and approach. Reframe change as an opportunity for growth, and set goals with built-in flexibility to accommodate unexpected shifts. Prioritize self-care to manage stress during transitions, communicate your needs to those around you, and stay organized with adaptable plans. This approach helps you maintain balance and effectively navigate both personal and professional changes.

Embracing Remote Work and Flexible Hours

The rise of remote work and flexible hours has transformed how we approach a work-life balance. With more control over when and where work is done, individuals can design a schedule that aligns with their personal lives. However, this flexibility also comes with its own set of challenges, such as the temptation to work beyond regular hours or difficulty separating work and home life.

Here's how to make the most of these opportunities:

1. Create a Dedicated Workspace: Whether working from home or in a shared space, having a dedicated area for work helps maintain a clear boundary between professional and personal life. Your workspace doesn't have to be an entire room; even a specific corner can signal to your mind that it's time to focus on work tasks.

2. Establish Clear Work Hours: One of the perks of flexible hours is choosing when you work best. However, it's important to set and communicate your work hours to prevent burnout and ensure colleagues or clients respect your time. Decide on a start and end time for your workday, and stick to it as much as possible to create a routine that supports balance.

3. Use Breaks Wisely: Flexible work allows you to integrate breaks throughout your day more naturally. Use these breaks to step away from your workspace, stretch, go for a walk, or engage in a hobby. Incorporating regular breaks can increase productivity and reduce stress, enhancing overall well-being.

4. Leverage Technology for Better Balance: Remote work often relies on digital tools to communicate and manage tasks. Use these tools not only to stay connected but also to set boundaries. Features like "Do Not Disturb" on messaging apps can help you focus during working hours and disconnect when your workday ends.

5. Experiment and Adjust: Finding the right balance

with flexible work arrangements takes some experimentation. Pay attention to what routines make you feel most productive and fulfilled. Don't be afraid to adjust your approach if something isn't working. The key is to remain open to change and continually refine your routine to meet your evolving needs.

Practical Tip: At the start of each workday, create a to-do list that outlines the most important tasks you need to complete. Rank these tasks by priority to help you stay focused and prevent the workday from spilling into personal time. This practice not only boosts productivity but also creates a natural endpoint for your workday, making it easier to disconnect and transition into your personal life.

Flexibility is not a one-time adjustment; it's an ongoing practice. By adopting a flexible mindset and developing strategies to adapt to changes, you create a more resilient approach to balancing work and life. Remote work and flexible hours offer unique opportunities to design a lifestyle that aligns with your priorities, but they require conscious effort to maintain boundaries and prevent burnout.

Remember, the goal of embracing flexibility and adaptation is to support a balanced life that feels both fulfilling and sustainable. As your needs and circumstances evolve, so will your approach to balance. By staying open to change and willing to adjust, you empower yourself to navigate life's complexities with greater ease and confidence.

CHAPTER 8: CREATING A BALANCED ROUTINE

Begin each workday by taking a few minutes to create a to-do list that includes everything you need to accomplish. Start by listing all the tasks you need to tackle, then categorize them based on urgency and importance. Use a system like the "Eisenhower Matrix," which divides tasks into four categories: urgent and important, important but not urgent, urgent but not important, and neither urgent nor important. This method helps you identify what needs your immediate attention versus what can be scheduled for later.

By ranking your tasks in order of priority, you establish a clear focus for your day, ensuring that you direct your energy toward the most critical activities first. This approach not only boosts productivity but also prevents less important tasks from consuming your time and mental resources. As you complete high-priority items, you'll find it easier to maintain momentum throughout the day without feeling overwhelmed.

Additionally, this structured to-do list creates a natural endpoint for your workday. Once you've completed the essential tasks, you'll have a sense of accomplishment that signals it's time to wind down and shift into personal time. This separation makes it easier to disconnect from work, reducing the temptation to continue working into your personal hours and helping you maintain a healthier work-life balance.

Crafting a Daily Routine That Works

Designing a daily routine that suits your unique lifestyle is crucial for achieving lasting balance. Structure your day with intention, prioritize tasks that align with both your personal and professional goals. Explore practical tips for time management, flexibility, and self-care that nurture your overall well-being.

1. Assessing Your Current Routine

The first step in creating a balanced routine is evaluating your current schedule. Understanding how you spend your time helps identify areas that need adjustment to achieve a better balance.

How to Assess Your Routine:

- Track Your Time: Keep a time log for a week, noting how you allocate your hours to work, personal activities, and rest.
- Identify Patterns: Look for patterns or time drains that impact your productivity or well-being. For example, do you find yourself working late into the evening or skipping meals?
- Evaluate Balance: Determine if your current routine effectively balances work, rest, and leisure. Are there areas where you feel overwhelmed or under-stimulated?

Practical Tip: Use a planner or digital calendar to track each activity. Allocate your time as evenly as possible to build a balanced schedule.

2. Setting Priorities and Goals

Establishing clear priorities and goals helps shape a routine that aligns with your values and aspirations. Define what is most important to you and ensure your routine reflects these priorities.

How to Set Priorities:

- Identify Key Areas: Determine the key areas of your life that require attention, such as work, family, health, and personal growth.
- Set Goals: Establish specific, achievable goals for each area. For example, if health is a priority, a goal might be to exercise for 30 minutes a day.
- Allocate Time: Assign dedicated time slots to work on these goals, integrating them into your daily routine.

Practical Tip: Create a list of your top priorities and allocate specific times for each. For instance, if family time and exercise are high priorities, schedule these activities into your day alongside work tasks.

3. Designing Your Ideal Routine

Create a daily routine that incorporates all aspects of your life, ensuring a balanced approach to work, rest, and leisure. Consider your personal preferences and responsibilities when designing your routine.

How to Design Your Routine:

- Morning Routine: Start your day with activities that set a positive tone. This might include exercise, breakfast, and planning your day.
- Work Blocks: Schedule focused work periods with regular breaks to maintain productivity and avoid burnout.
- Personal Time: Allocate time for personal activities, such as hobbies, socializing, or relaxation, to ensure a well-

rounded routine.

- Evening Routine: Wind down with activities that help you relax and prepare for a restful night's sleep, such as reading or meditating.

Practical Tip: When designing your ideal routine, begin by adding just one or two new habits at a time. For instance, if you want to start your mornings with exercise, set aside 10 minutes for a short workout or stretch. Once this becomes a habit, gradually introduce other elements, like a breakfast ritual or morning planning. Building your routine step-by-step prevents overwhelm, increases the likelihood of long-term success, and allows you to adjust as you discover what works best for your lifestyle.

Incorporating Work, Rest, and Leisure

Achieving true balance requires more than just managing work; it involves making time for rest and leisure too. Delve into the art of blending productivity with relaxation, highlighting how breaks and enjoyable activities can recharge your energy and enhance focus. Learn how to create a well-rounded routine that values downtime as much as work, fostering a more sustainable and fulfilling lifestyle.

1. Balancing Work and Rest

A balanced routine includes both productive work periods and adequate rest. This balance is essential for maintaining energy levels and avoiding burnout.

How to Balance Work and Rest:

- Scheduled Breaks: Implement regular breaks during

work hours to rest and recharge. For example, take a 10-minute break every hour to stretch or step away from your workspace.

- Rest Periods: Ensure you have dedicated rest periods throughout the day, including a lunch break and time for relaxation.
- Work Limits: Set clear boundaries for your work hours to prevent work from encroaching on personal time.

Practical Tip: Incorporate the Pomodoro Technique into your routine to ensure a balanced approach to work and rest. Work in focused 25-minute intervals, followed by a 5-minute break. After four work intervals, take a longer break of 15-30 minutes. This method not only boosts productivity by encouraging deep focus but also provides regular, structured rest periods to keep your energy levels high and prevent burnout.

2. Allocating Time for Leisure

Leisure activities are vital for rejuvenation and personal fulfillment. Incorporate leisure time into your routine to enjoy activities that bring you joy and relaxation.

How to Allocate Time for Leisure:

- Plan Leisure Activities: Schedule regular leisure activities, such as hobbies, outings, or social events, to ensure you make time for enjoyable experiences.
- Be Spontaneous: Allow some flexibility in your routine for spontaneous leisure activities, giving yourself the freedom to explore new interests and experiences.
- Balance Obligations and Fun: Ensure that leisure activities are balanced with other obligations, preventing them from becoming a source of stress or guilt.

Practical Tip: Treat leisure time with the same importance as work meetings or appointments by scheduling dedicated 'leisure block' on your calendar. Choose specific times during the week for activities you love, like reading, gardening, or catching up with friends. By blocking out this time in advance, you're more likely to honor it and can enjoy these moments guilt-free, knowing they're part of your well-rounded routine.

The Importance of Self- Care and Hobbies

Self-care and hobbies are vital components of a balanced life, providing an essential break from daily demands and nurturing mental and emotional health. Prioritizing activities that bring joy and relaxation can reduce stress, boost creativity, and improve overall well-being. Embracing personal interests is not a luxury but a necessary practice for maintaining harmony between work and life.

1. Prioritizing Self-Care

Self-care is a crucial component of a balanced routine, focusing on activities that promote physical, mental, and emotional well-being. Prioritizing self-care helps you maintain balance and resilience.

How to Prioritize Self-Care:

- Create a Self-Care Plan: Develop a self-care plan that includes activities such as exercise, healthy eating, mindfulness practices, and adequate sleep.
- Schedule Self-Care Time: Integrate self-care activities into your daily routine, treating them as essential commitments rather than optional extras.

- Monitor Your Well-Being: Regularly assess your physical and emotional well-being to ensure your self-care practices are effective and adjust as needed.

Practical Tip: Identify self-care activities that resonate with you, such as yoga or journaling. Schedule these activities into your routine to ensure they are consistently practiced.

2. Embracing Hobbies

Hobbies provide an outlet for creativity and relaxation, enriching your life and contributing to a balanced routine. Engaging in hobbies helps you unwind and brings a sense of fulfillment.

How to Embrace Hobbies:

- Explore Interests: Identify hobbies or interests that bring you joy and explore new activities to discover what you enjoy most.
- Incorporate Hobbies into Your Routine: Set aside dedicated time for hobbies, ensuring they become a regular part of your schedule.
- Share with Others: Share your hobbies with friends or family to create social connections and enhance the enjoyment of your activities.

Practical Tip: When incorporating a new hobby into your routine, start with small, manageable goals. For example, if you're learning to paint, aim for a 15-minute painting session a couple of times a week. This approach prevents hobbies from feeling overwhelmed or like another obligation. As you progress, gradually increase the time or complexity of your hobby to keep it enjoyable and rewarding.

By crafting a balanced daily routine that includes work, rest, and leisure, and prioritizing self-care and hobbies, you can achieve a harmonious work-life balance that supports your overall well-being. This balanced approach helps you manage daily responsibilities while also enjoying personal fulfillment and relaxation.

CHAPTER 9:
MONITORING AND
ADJUSTING YOUR
BALANCE

Creating a work-life balance is not something you can set and forget; it's a dynamic, ongoing process that requires conscious effort and regular reassessment. Life is full of changes— personal responsibilities shift, career demands fluctuate, and new challenges arise. What worked for you last month may no longer suit your current situation. That's why it's crucial to view work-life balance as a flexible, evolving goal rather than a fixed state.

In this chapter, we'll explore how to routinely check in with yourself and your routine to ensure it aligns with your current needs and priorities. This involves assessing how you're spending your time, identifying areas of stress or imbalance, and adjusting where necessary. We'll discuss practical ways to set boundaries, how to adapt when unexpected changes occur, and methods for integrating self-care into your everyday routine.

Additionally, we'll look at how to adopt a mindset of continuous improvement, which includes learning from setbacks or periods of imbalance. By reflecting on what didn't work, you can refine your approach and make more informed decisions moving forward. Embracing this mindset helps you stay proactive and resilient, allowing you to maintain a healthier, more adaptable approach to both work and personal life. Developing these habits of regular evaluation and adjustment ensures that your work-life balance remains in tune with your evolving goals and circumstances.

Regular Check-Ins and Adjustments

◆ ◆ ◆

To maintain a harmonious work-life balance, it's crucial to pause and reflect on how well your current routine serves you. This process of self-reflection helps you identify areas where your work-life balance might be slipping and highlights any adjustments that need to be made. It's also an opportunity to celebrate what is working well, which can provide motivation to keep up positive habits. Consider setting aside time—weekly, monthly, or quarterly—to review your balance.

During these check-ins, ask yourself the following questions:

- Am I meeting my personal and professional goals? Reflect on whether your daily routine allows you to make progress in both areas. If you're excelling at work but neglecting self-care, family, or personal interests, it's time to make changes.
- How do I feel emotionally and physically? Listen to your body and mind. Frequent stress, exhaustion, or feelings of being overwhelmed are signs that your balance might be off. If you notice burnout symptoms, act to re-prioritize rest and relaxation.
- Am I sticking to my boundaries? Evaluate whether you're respecting the boundaries you set around work and personal time. If you find yourself frequently working late or checking emails during family time, consider ways to reinforce those limits.

Practical Tip: Set SMART (Specific, Measurable, Achievable, Relevant, Time-bound) goals for your balance initiatives. This clarity will help you measure progress and make targeted adjustments.

Once you've completed your check-in, it's time to adjust. For example, if you find that your work is creeping into personal time, consider revisiting your work boundaries. This might mean reaffirming your set work hours or scheduling breaks more intentionally throughout the day. If you're noticing a lack of time for hobbies or social activities, look at where you can trim non-essential tasks or delegate responsibilities to free up time.

Flexibility is key here. Life rarely goes according to a strict plan, so being adaptable and willing to experiment with changes is vital. You might try incorporating small adjustments first to see their impact. For instance, if you're struggling with exhaustion, you might start by ending your workday 30 minutes earlier a few times a week and using that time for a restful activity. If this change has a positive effect, you can consider making it a regular part of your routine.

Learning from Setbacks

Setbacks are a natural part of any journey toward balance. They provide valuable learning opportunities that can help you refine your approach and enhance your resilience. Embracing setbacks with a growth mindset enables you to turn challenges into steppingstones.

1. Analyze the Root Causes

When setbacks occur, it's essential to analyze their root causes. Reflect on what led to the setback and how it impacted your balance. Understanding the underlying issues helps in developing effective strategies to address similar challenges in the future.

- Reflect Without Judgment: When things go off track, avoid self-criticism. Reflect on what happened with a compassionate mindset. What caused the setback? Was it a situation beyond your control, or were there actions you could have taken differently? Understanding the root causes helps you prepare for similar challenges in the future.

Practical Tip: After experiencing a setback, take time to journal about the situation. Identify the factors that contributed to the issue and brainstorm potential solutions or preventative measures.

2. Develop Resilience Strategies

Building resilience involves preparing yourself mentally and emotionally to handle setbacks effectively. This might include developing stress management techniques, fostering a support network, or cultivating a positive outlook. Resilience helps you recover from setbacks more quickly and return to your balanced state.

- Develop Coping Strategies: Use setbacks as a chance to build resilience. If you encounter a particularly stressful period at work, explore stress-management techniques like mindfulness, exercise, or time-blocking to prevent burnout in the future. Having strategies in place can help you bounce back more quickly when life throws you a curveball.

Practical Tip: Incorporate resilience-building practices into your daily routine, such as mindfulness meditation or regular exercise. These practices can enhance your ability to cope with stress and maintain balance during challenging times.

3. Seek Support and Guidance

Don't hesitate to seek support or guidance when facing setbacks. Talking to a mentor, coach, or trusted friend can provide valuable perspectives and advice. External support can offer fresh insights and help you navigate difficult situations more effectively.

- Adjust Your Plan: After reflecting on the setback, revise your routine or strategies. If an overly packed schedule caused burnout, try incorporating more breaks into your day. If a lack of boundaries led to excessive work hours, practice setting firm limits and communicating them clearly with colleagues and family. The key is to make realistic changes that support a healthier balance moving forward.

Practical Tip: Identify a network of individuals who can offer guidance and support during setbacks. Schedule regular check-ins with these individuals to discuss challenges and seek advice.

Continuous Improvement

Achieving work-life balance is a dynamic process that thrives on continuous improvement. By adopting a mindset of ongoing growth, you can more easily adapt to new challenges and changing circumstances. The idea isn't to strive for perfection but to consistently seek ways to enhance your balance in small, manageable steps.

1. Embrace a Growth Mindset

Approach your balance efforts with a growth mindset, which emphasizes the belief that abilities and strategies can be developed through effort and learning. This mindset encourages you to view challenges as opportunities for growth and to persist in your efforts to improve.

- Celebrate Small Wins: Recognize and celebrate the progress you make, no matter how small. Each adjustment, boundary set, or new habit formed is a step toward a more balanced life. Celebrating these achievements boosts motivation and reinforces the positive changes you're implementing.

Practical Tip: Practice self-compassion and celebrate small victories along the way. Recognizing your progress reinforces positive behaviors and motivates you to continue striving for balance.

2. Stay Informed and Adapt

Stay informed about new techniques, tools, and research related to work-life balance. Being open to new ideas and adapting your approach ensures that you're utilizing the most effective strategies for your unique situation.

- Keep Learning: Stay informed about new strategies, tools, and techniques that can support work-life balance. Read books, take courses, or join groups focused on personal development and well-being. Continuous learning helps you discover fresh ideas to integrate into your routine.

Practical Tip: Subscribe to relevant blogs, attend workshops, or participate in webinars to stay updated on best practices for work-life balance. Incorporate new insights into your routine as appropriate.

3. Review and Refine Your Strategies

Periodically review your balance strategies and assess their effectiveness. Adjust based on your experiences, feedback, and evolving needs. Continuous refinement helps you stay aligned with your goals and ensures that your balance remains dynamic and adaptable.

- Embrace Flexibility: Continuous improvement also means remaining flexible. As your life evolves, so will your definition of balance. Be open to changing your goals and strategies as needed. What worked well during one phase of life might not suit another, so regularly reassess your priorities and adjust accordingly.

Practical Tip: Set aside time each quarter to review your balance strategies. Evaluate what's working well and what could be improved and implement changes to enhance your overall harmony.

Regular check-ins and adjustments are essential for maintaining a healthy work-life balance. By routinely reflecting on your routine and making necessary changes, you can ensure that your schedule continues to align with your evolving needs and priorities. The process of evaluating, learning from setbacks, and making informed adjustments fosters a mindset of continuous improvement, allowing you to stay adaptable and proactive in achieving balance. With these habits in place, you'll be better equipped to create a routine that supports both your professional success and personal fulfillment.

Remember, the journey to balance isn't about achieving a perfect state—it's about consistently striving to create a life that feels fulfilling and manageable. Embrace the small adjustments, learn from challenges, and celebrate your progress along the way. In doing so, you'll be well-equipped to navigate the demands of work and life with greater ease, confidence, and joy.

CONCLUSION

Achieving a balanced life isn't about sticking rigidly to a flawless routine; rather, it's about creating a sense of harmony that adapts to life's inevitable fluctuations. Life is unpredictable, and trying to force it into a strict schedule can lead to stress and burnout. True balance comes from the ability to shift and adjust your habits and routines as your personal and professional circumstances evolve. It's about being present, recognizing when things are out of sync, and taking proactive steps to restore equilibrium.

Throughout this guide, we've delved into a variety of strategies to lay the groundwork for a sustainable work-life balance. We began by examining the importance of self-awareness—understanding your current habits, strengths, and areas that might need improvement. By knowing where your time and energy go, you gain clarity on what might be disrupting your balance and what changes could help you regain control. From there, we explored the significance of setting boundaries, such as creating clear distinctions between work and personal time. Establishing these boundaries is key to preventing work from encroaching on your relaxation and leisure, allowing you to be fully present in each area of your life.

Managing stress is another vital element. We've discussed practical techniques to help you cope with daily pressures, whether through mindfulness practices, exercise, or simply setting aside time for self-care. Embracing flexibility was also a central theme. Life is rarely linear, and unexpected events or new responsibilities can throw your routine off course. By adopting a flexible mindset and being willing to adjust your approach, you can navigate these changes more smoothly, without feeling like you've failed or lost control.

Now, it's time to integrate these elements into a holistic lifestyle that supports both your personal and professional well-being. Achieving harmony involves blending these strategies into a routine that feels natural and sustainable for you. It's not about ticking off a checklist of tasks each day, but rather about finding a rhythm that works in your current phase of life. Some days, balance might mean prioritizing work because of an important project, while on other days, it may involve focusing on rest, family, or personal interests.

The key is to stay mindful and regularly assess how your routine aligns with your needs and priorities. When you notice signs of imbalance—such as chronic stress, fatigue, or a lack of fulfillment —view it as a signal to revisit your strategies and adjust. By doing so, you can create a lifestyle that evolves with you, ensuring that your pursuit of balance remains both realistic and empowering. In this way, you can step confidently into a life that nurtures your well-being, allowing you to thrive in both your personal and professional endeavors.

Embracing a Balanced Life

◆ ◆ ◆

Embracing balance means giving yourself permission to be adaptable and forgiving. There will be times when work demands more of your energy, and other moments when personal matters take precedence. The key is to remain mindful of these shifts and adjust as needed, understanding that balance is a fluid process rather than a fixed state.

Start by recognizing that self-care, personal growth, and meaningful connections are just as important as professional success. Balance is about aligning your daily actions with your values and goals, ensuring that you make time for what truly matters. This might involve reshaping your routine, setting clearer boundaries, or simply taking a moment each day to reflect on your well-being.

Remember, setbacks and challenges are natural. They offer opportunities for learning and growth, allowing you to refine your approach and build resilience. By regularly checking in with yourself, adapting to change, and celebrating your progress, you develop a stronger foundation for balance that can sustain you through life's ups and downs.

A balanced life isn't a destination to be reached; it's a lifelong journey of self-discovery and continual adjustment. As you move forward, stay committed to the practices that support your harmony. Whether it's prioritizing rest, nurturing relationships, or pursuing passions outside of work, these small yet significant choices will help you maintain a healthier, more fulfilling lifestyle.

In embracing a balanced life, you create space for joy, purpose, and personal growth. You build a life that not only meets the demands of your career but also allows you to thrive as an individual. This journey is yours to shape, with each day offering a new opportunity to create a balance that feels right for you.

Thank you for taking the time to read Mastering Balance: A Modern Guide to Harmonizing Work and Life. I truly appreciate your trust in exploring this journey with me, and I hope the insights and strategies provided have inspired you to create a more balanced and fulfilling life.

It's not always easy to find harmony between work and personal life, but taking the steps to understand, adapt, and nurture your well-being is a powerful investment in yourself. I hope this book has given you the tools, motivation, and reassurance needed to take charge of your balance and make it work for you.

Your journey to balance is unique and ongoing, and I'm grateful to have been a part of it. May the lessons here support you in achieving a lifestyle that brings you peace, joy, and a renewed sense of purpose. Here's to a future filled with balance, growth, and the things that matter most. Thank you once again, and I wish you all the best on this rewarding path forward!

*DISCLAIMER: I am not a psychiatrist, therapist, doctor, or mental health professional. I am not offering to diagnose, treat, or prevent any medical or mental health conditions. The information in this e-book is not a replacement for professional advice.

ABOUT THE AUTHOR

Nicole Varela Rodriguez

Nicole Rodriguez is a versatile author known for her motivational and personal growth writings.

Alongside her writing, she runs a successful mobile notary business. In her downtime, she loves to travel, explore unique hotels, and check out hidden culinary gems with her food-blogging husband and their two teenage boys.

Based in East Palo Alto, California, Nicole holds a Bachelor's in Philosophy from Santa Clara University.

To learn more about her journey, visit:
www.riquezabusinessventures.com

Made in the USA
Columbia, SC
16 November 2024

46684077R00043